AS I
REMEMBER

AS I
REMEMBER

A STORY OF THE LIFE OF BENNIE ORR JONES

JANA JONES WOODALL

Charleston, SC
www.PalmettoPublishing.com

As I Remember

First Edition

Paperback ISBN: 978-1-63837-695-8

Acknowledgments

*As in all things in life I am inspired and grateful for the love of God.
Without Him and His promise for eternal salvation, we have nothing.*

*This book was inspired by the encouragement of my dear loving husband,
Ed Woodall. He is my rock. The history of Dad's life has always in-
trigued him and felt it worthy of documenting, if for nothing more than
future generations to know their heritage.*

*Thanks to my sisters, Lynette Thompson and Jaren Robertson, for being
sweet, loving sisters and providing information and editing for this
labor of love.
And lastly, thanks to my parents for a lifetime of unconditional
love and support!*

Jana Jones Woodall

TABLE OF CONTENTS

CHAPTER 1

WHERE IT ALL BEGAN

This story began in a small town in south Georgia named Nahunta. Nahunta, originally called Victoria, was founded about 1870. There are two beliefs on how this town was renamed, but the origin of the name has never been officially verified. One belief was that it was renamed in 1899 for timber executive N.A. Hunter, who was of Indian descent. The Iroquoian (Tuscarora) Indian word Nahunta is thought to mean "tall trees". A second belief is the town was renamed by a turpentine producer who came from Nahunta, North Carolina.

In 1923, the seat of Brantley County, named after Benjamin D. Brantley, was transferred to Nahunta from Hoboken. Today's population of Brantley County is approximately 19,000. (1)

CHAPTER 2

THE JONES FAMILY HISTORY

My paternal great grandfather, Benjamin Franklin "Frank" Jones, was born in 1859 on a farm in Lulaton just outside Nahunta. He was the fourth child of Harley Jones and Dora Knox Jones.

Farm life changed when Frank was about two years old with the beginning of the Civil War in 1861. In March 1862, Harley Jones volunteered to serve in the 26th Georgia Infantry Regiment and was elected Lieutenant in his company. Preparations were underway for the 26th Georgia to leave for Virginia as soon as possible. Being elected an officer, Harley was allowed to have a "body servant" to travel with him to Virginia and stay with him. The "body servant" was a young slave named Steve. At the appointed time, Lieutenant Jones and Steve said goodbye to family and farm and left for Virginia. Frank Jones was then about three years old when he said goodbye to his father.

Things went badly for Lieutenant Jones in Virginia when he became ill and left the ranks near Gordonsville, Virginia. He was admitted to a Confederate hospital in Gordonsville where he died of typhoid on August 30, 1862. Lieutenant Jones had been in the Confederate Army for only five months. He is buried in a cemetery in Gordonsville, Virginia.

Lieutenant Jones's body servant, Steve, was now a long way from southeast Georgia and alone, which was a bad situation for a slave to be in at that time. He began to walk south from Gordonsville, Virginia to Georgia and continued all the way to Lulaton, which he called home. When he crossed the Satilla River near Lulaton it must have been like crossing the Jordan River into the Promised Land. What a welcome sight for Steve as he crossed the field towards the house. Traveling alone, he was watched by Harley's wife Dora and as well as Owen, Mary Jane, Elizabeth, and Frank. They knew then that Harley Jones would not return.

Later life would take another turn for Frank when his mother would marry Mose Highsmith. He was a good man who would raise the children as his own. Frank passed through childhood and into young adulthood enjoying the things that a young man enjoyed at that time. In Frank's own words; "I lived at ease nor feared to die. Never thought of anything else, only a big-time in the pleasures of this world".

In mid-1883 Frank Jones married Molly Knox. The following year a daughter was born to Frank and Molly. Her name was Mamie Jones or "Auntie" as we came to know her. I remember visiting her in her large home in Nahunta which is now known as Frye Funeral Home.

All did not go well and Molly died as a result of childbirth. Little Mamie was taken by Molly Knox's family to their home in Hickox (a small community just south of Nahunta). With a very troubled mind that resulted from the death of his wife Molly, Frank turned to Old Smyrna Church, as he called it, for help. He had been attending Smyrna Church all his life but now with a more positive outlook.

Soon thereafter, Frank met Melissa Herrin. On one occasion Frank visited Melissa's home to speak to her father. He said "Mr. Herrin, I would like to marry one of your daughters." Mr. Herrin yelled upstairs, "which one of you girls wants to marry Frank Jones?" Little Melissa appeared at the head of the stairs and said "I do". On February 1, 1886, Frank and Melissa were married in Wayne County Georgia. Melissa had eleven children and with Mamie Jones from Frank's first wife they had twelve total - seven boys and five girls. Frank's 5th child born in 1892 was my Papa, Daniel LaFayette Jones.

In early 1931 an unusual event took place on the Frank Jones farm. An airplane landed in the large field near the house due to unknown reasons. Because of the soft soil it landed in, it had gone over on its nose bending the propeller. Two men were in the airplane and were not hurt in the landing. Melissa Jones was home alone and stepped outside to see what was happening. At that time, or shortly thereafter, Melissa Jones suffered a stroke and was taken back into the house by the men from the airplane. All the family members were notified and gathered at her bedside and outside on the porch. Nothing could be done and Melissa Herrin Jones died January 5, 1931. She is buried in the graveyard at Smyrna Church. The men with the airplane remained until after attending the funeral, made repairs to their plane and flew away.

Later, Frank Jones married his third wife, Cora Prescott of Charlton County. They continued to live on the farm for a few years and then moved into a home in Lulaton.

Frank Jones stayed in the area and became Pastor of Smyrna Church. He died on July 22, 1944 and was buried beside his second wife Melissa. Families would put away good cypress board over a period of time, saving them until the need arose for a coffin. Those talented in woodwork would build the coffin. Frank's wooden coffin was made by his son Harley with the help of the other sons. (2)

CHAPTER 3

THE PARENTS

Flossie Marie Orr was Dad's mother who was born and grew up in Wapakoneta, Ohio until she was in her teens and moved with her family to south Georgia. It is believed that Flossie may have graduated high school in Ohio just prior to the family moving south. Some of her school books, a set of encyclopedias, her mother Ida's purse, champagne glasses and a sewing machine are amongst some of my prized possessions.

The Orr family, consisting of Dr. Orr, his wife Ida and children Flossie and Calvin, followed other Ohioans that had settled in the south Georgia area. The Orrs first settled in Nahunta then moved to Hoboken where Flossie's father, Dr. Jerome Orr, the area veterinarian, became the first mayor of Hoboken. Not long after the county seat was created in Hoboken it soon moved to Nahunta. During the recent 100th celebration of the beginning of the county seat, Dad heard his grandfather, Dr. Orr, mentioned as being a past mayor. My Dad has a top hat which belonged to the Orr family.

Flossie's only sibling was a younger brother named Calvin. He was talented in many ways. He was good at training animals such as chickens and dogs. Maybe that is where Dad got his ability to train hunting dogs. Calvin was also very artistic. He died of blood poisoning at the young age of 18.

The family later moved to Fort Lauderdale, Florida where Dr. Orr tried his hand in real estate due to the housing boom in the area in the 1920s. Moving south ended up being a losing proposition so the family returned to south Georgia. Dad later found a Bill of Sale which indicated Dr. Orr returned to Georgia to sell cars in Waycross.

Sometime in the late 1910s, Flossie met my grandfather Daniel LaFayette Jones. Flossie was living in Hoboken, 10 miles west of Nahunta, with her parents and brother.

Dad does not know how Flossie and Dan met. They married in Hoboken on March 12, 1918. Papa, as we referred to Dan, was in some way employed in the timber business at that time. He was not a finished carpenter, but he built Flossie a house after they were married. The house was a spacious, wooden two story house. It had 4 bedrooms, a foyer, living room, dining room and an eat in kitchen. At this time there was an out house, but an indoor bathroom was added later. There were porches on the front and back and a separate garage at the end of the driveway. This house would one day also be my home.

CHAPTER 4

ALL BOYS

In 1922, Flossie and Dan began their family by having Sibert LaFayette Jones. On January 23, 1926, my father Bennie 'Ben' Orr Jones was born and named after his grandfather Benjamin Franklin Jones. His birth certificate says Benny. He assumes the doctor spelled it incorrectly because his Mom went with Bennie. Last but not least, in 1928, Joseph Valree Jones arrived. All three of Flossie and Dan's boys were born at home with the help of Dr. Moore, one of two doctors, who practiced in the small town.

The family had a few Christmas traditions as kids. One was the three boys would go with their parents before Christmas to cut down a pine tree in the woods to decorate. Also, in addition to receiving a few gifts from their parents, they would also wrap a trinket or something small they already had for each of their brothers. Something they all would get a laugh out of on Christmas morning.

During the 1920s, Dan Jones, my Papa, owned the Chevrolet dealership in Nahunta. The dealership was located at the northeast corner of what is now Highway 301 and US 84. It was operated by J. Morris Highsmith. You could also buy a Ford in the building where Brantley Gas is now located. Nahunta lost both of their dealerships during the Depression.

Flossie had a 1929 Chevrolet and traded it for a 1936 Chevrolet. It was the first year of automobiles having hydraulic brakes. Not being used to the new brakes and having no seat belts in the car, Flossie almost threw them all through the windshield leaving the dealership. This was the car she used to go to Waycross shopping.

Gas pumps were quite different when Dad was a boy. Using a hand pump, you pumped a certain amount of fuel into a glass cylinder then gravity allowed it to flow into the car's gas tank. Gas in Waycross around that time was 16 cents a gallon.

CHAPTER 5

THE EARLY YEARS

Dad's early years were not just work as there was always time for fun and games. When he was about 10 years old, he went fishing on an old wooden bridge where the auto parts store is now. As most any young man would, you drop your line and figure out once you catch a fish how you are going to pull it up through the crack in the bridge. He caught a fish which was too big to pull through the crack. After tying off his line, he went to the nearby service station and borrowed an ax from the late Mr. Pat Stokes. Dad cut a hole big enough to retrieve his fish. That hole remained in the bridge as long as it was there.

On his way to school in the mornings, if Dad had a penny in his pocket he would stop at the Petty store for five silver bells or Hershey Kisses as we know them today. This would make his day.

Dad's entrepreneurial ideas began at an early age. He had numerous ideas for making his own money. One idea led him to search through trash piles for used medicine bottles. Maybe that is the yester-year's method of dumpster diving. After washing them he would sell them for one cent each to the two doctors who were in Nahunta at that time and they would use the medicine bottles again.

Dad also had a shoeshine business. He made his own wooden box that a man could put his foot on for his shoes to be shined. He bought his supplies at the local store and kept them inside the wooden box. He would hang out at Roy Ham's Barber shop waiting on the next man that had a nickel to spare for a good shoe shine.

Dad's next business was selling peanuts. He would buy raw peanuts at the local store. At home he would parch the peanuts in the oven of his family's wood-burning stove. He would put 40 peanuts in a bag and would sell them at any event in town where there were large gatherings. However, most of his peanut sales took place at the high school basketball games. He wandered all over the gym selling his peanut bags for a nickel each.

Dad had finally saved enough money to buy a brand new bicycle for $18. This bicycle afforded him the opportunity for another venture to earn money. He delivered the Florida Times Union to 12 customers who lived in town. He completed his paper route each morning before going to school.

For entertainment, Dad and other kids played marbles. I played marbles when I was young as well. I can remember boys in elementary school trading marbles to have an assortment of colors and designs.

Having no television at the time, traveling movie shows were a welcomed entertainment. The show traveled from town to town showing black-and-white silent movies. The words were shown on the screen. Dad would go when the movie was in town and pay 10 cents for admission. During the winter there would be an open barrel fire inside the tent to keep them warm.

CHAPTER 6

THE TEEN YEARS

Papa started his own sawmill in the early 1940s after the Chevrolet dealership went bankrupt. The lumber from the sawmill was sold to businesses in Jacksonville, Florida, Waycross, Georgia and locals, to build barns and houses. All three of Papa's boys worked in the sawmill at one time or another. The sawmill was located about one mile east of Nahunta just off of Highway 84 which is now Highway 82.

Dad began helping Papa in the sawmill when he was about 12 years old. They would cut trees, gather and load the logs for transport to the sawmill. There was one particular day in 1941 they would never forget. Dad was about 15 years old at the time. Papa and the boys were north of Raybon, a small community just north of Nahunta. Papa had gone into the swamp to cut pine trees. There was a ditch full of water where the boys floated the logs back to the truck. They also used oxen to help move the logs. (More about the oxen later.) Uncle Sibert had his driver's license so he had taken the truck into town. When he got there he found out his mother, Flossie, had had a stroke. He went back to the work site and picked up his Dad and brothers to check on her. She had no paralysis but her health was never the same, declining slowly. She lived almost a year and died in 1942. She asked Dad to make her a promise - never smoke or drink. With the exception of a one time beer tasting, he has always kept that promise to his mother.

An interesting thing Dad could add to his resume was ox rider. Papa had purchased oxen named Buck, Bully, Broad and Golden from a man in Hickox. The oxen were kept in an ox lot (pen) at Papa's house. When needed the oxen would be used to pull logs around at the sawmill or at a tree cutting site. When not used for a while the oxen would be turned loose to graze on grass. After a while they would wander back to the man's house in Hickox where they were raised. The man would pen them up until Dad went to get them. Their past owner didn't mind. When they were needed for work again Papa would take Dad out of school to go to Hickox. He would climb on Buck's back and ride him back home. Bully, Broad and Golden would follow them.

During this period in history, sawmills moved to where the timber needed cutting. Unlike today, the sawmill stays put and the logs are trucked in. Papa's mill was first run by steam engine, then a diesel engine and they had also run it with an auto engine. In addition to sawing logs for structures, they sawed logs to make shingles. The shingle mill was run separately. Each sawmill employee was paid wages of one dollar per day.

In making lumber out of the trees, the trees would first be put through the sawmill to slice off the bark. Four slices were made around the tree for this removal. Thin wood pieces could then be cut out of these slabs as needed and the remainder with the bark still intact would be thrown into a large scrap pile. When Dad and his brothers received inquiries from area residents about needing firewood, they would load up the large bed of papa's truck and deliver the scrap wood. Since they were not paid for their work at the mill, Dad and his brothers were happy to share the two dollars per load that they were paid.

The sawmill stayed in existence up until 1943 or 1944. World War II had been going on for several years. Many of the young men were involved in the war and Papa could not get the hired help to keep the mill running. During that time, Highway 301 was getting more populated. Motels were being built along the highway. Papa took a job in construction and helped in building businesses and especially the growing number of motels. The building boom really started when the war was over.

As Dad grew older, he also played basketball and had a hoop attached to the garage at Papa's house. They used an eight inch rubber ball. Dad, Claude Smith and others spent their spare time under that hoop. They had clay courts to play on at school. It was a luxury when the first indoor basketball gym was built and many could enjoy the sport. There was no television so many kids were active in sports and outdoor play.

The new indoor basketball court was a big improvement compared to the outdoor clay court. The county did not pay for the indoor court. The townspeople donated the logs and manpower to build it. It was a good gym with hardwood floors. After the war, Dad and his friends had a really good team. They were so good that it was suggested they should disperse some of their players to other teams, so the other teams would have a chance to beat them. They never split up.

CHAPTER 7

EDUCATION

Dad attended Nahunta schools and for the most part was a good student. My sister Lynette and I later attended the same elementary school as Dad. One wing of it was still standing recently and slated for renovation until it burned on February 23, 2021.

In high school Dad began to fail. Then came his first big mistake. He quit school in 9th grade. Dad wrote some of his memories down and this is one of his quotes. "My advice to students, if you feel your grades are slipping don't be bashful about it, admit it and keep asking the teacher for extra help until you understand the problem. Most teachers are willing to do a little extra to help a sincere student." (3)

Dad's shortened education was surprising to me. He had owned and/or managed his own businesses as long as I could remember. He made a good living to keep us comfortable. Dad never seemed to struggle in the management of his businesses. He did tell me he felt his vocabulary was lacking, but who knew?! When I was in school I found some of his report cards and brought to his attention his less than stellar grades in high school hoping it would provide leverage with my own grades if I ever needed it. It was obvious he was not proud of them and expected better from his girls.

CHAPTER 8

LIFE WITH HIS BROTHERS

Dad said he and his brothers got along well with seldom an altercation. Seems a bit unusual for three boys close in age. Flossie was the disciplinarian and kept a pretty close check on them. She never objected to Dad quitting school as she was very sick by then.

Papa only spanked Dad once that he recalled and he is not sure why. He did recall his brother Sibert getting in trouble. They were in Fort Lauderdale visiting his grandparents. There were grapefruit trees all around. While inside the house Sibert said something Papa didn't approve of and he thumped him on the head. A few minutes later Sibert was outside, up a grapefruit tree looking back inside through a window at them. They all laughed at him keeping his distance to stay out of trouble.

After Uncle Sibert graduated high school he moved to north Georgia, close to the Tennessee line, and got a job. He stayed with friends that had previously lived in Nahunta. Dad thought his reason for leaving was probably to get away from the sawmill work.

Dad and his brothers were in some way or another fighting the war at the same time. Uncle Sibert was a merchant seaman in the Merchant Marines. He captained a boat in The Mediterranean Sea shuttling supplies. Dad was in the Merchant Marines and Army and Uncle Joe was in the Navy. It must have been hard for Papa having them all gone to war at the same time, especially after losing his wife just a few years earlier.

CHAPTER 9

WORLD WAR II

World War II began September 1, 1939. There were 18 shipyards in the United States building Liberty ships to haul supplies and equipment to our forces overseas. One of those shipyards was in Brunswick, Georgia just 36 miles east of Nahunta. Each ship cost $2 million dollars to build. Adjusted for inflation, today each ship would cost approximately $39 million dollars. 2,751 were built from 1941-1945 at different shipyards around the United States. A ship would carry a crew of civilian merchant seamen as well as naval personnel to operate defensive guns and communications equipment. There were no mine detection devices on the ships at that time.

Dad, who was 17 years old, worked at the shipyard in Brunswick for a year or less building Liberty ships. He still lived at home and traveled to Brunswick daily catching rides with others since he had no car. One of those gracious enough to give him a ride was Judge Rodenberry's brother. Dad said his driving was hell on wheels. There was a couple living with Papa and his family at that time. The man worked at the shipyard so Dad would ride with him some as well.

Dad was considered a "burner" at the shipyard. Ship fitters laid out what they needed in the form of pipes or metal and the burner would cut it. It was hot work and sometimes done in the bilge. When there was little work to do they would lie down in front of electric fans to cool off. Unbeknownst to Dad, he would one day be sailing on the Liberty ships he was helping build.

THE MERCHANT MARINES

In 1943, still at the age of 17, Dad joined the Merchant Marines as a merchant seaman and helped sail the Liberty ships until after the war. To train as a merchant seaman, Dad took a train to St. Petersburg, Florida. During training only, they wore Navy sailor uniforms, but during cruises they wore civilian clothes. The seamen were put up in hotels and trained for six weeks. They had classroom training, as well as marching and drills where Dad was a squad leader of 10 men. Hands-on training was completed by taking a train to New York where they boarded an older coal fired Liberty ship and sailed to Norfolk, Virginia. With training complete, Dad took a train to Nahunta, stayed for a few days but soon reported to the Union in Jacksonville for assignment of his first voyage.

The seamen worked an 8 hour shift at their assigned duties. The other 16 hours they had free time with the exception of their on-call assignment to an onboard Navy gunner. The enemy made attempts to destroy the convoys prior to them reaching their destination. Should an alarm sound and an attack imminent, those seamen not working their assigned shift would report immediately to their preassigned Navy gunner to assist.

Dad traveled by train from Nahunta to Jacksonville, Florida where he embarked on the ships that were already loaded. Between sailings he could take off a day for every week at sea, which was the maximum time allowed to not be drafted. Dad usually took 5-10 days off before signing up for his next cruise. The Merchant Marine pay was better than the Army was paying.

Once the ships were loaded with supplies and crew, they sailed to New York to meet up with many other ships including two destroyer escorts from England. A convoy of about 80 Liberty ships slowly traveled to England, 4 abreast, with the destroyer escorts moving around them. If a destroyer escort flew a black flag, it meant they were seeing something that could be enemy submarines. Many times it was just big fish. However, you could never let your guard down. Out of the 2,751 Liberty ships that sailed during World War II approximately 200 were sunk.

Once while traveling in the convoy, the ship Dad was on broke down. The convoy kept moving and the disabled ship was on its own. The ship was repaired and they caught up with the convoy in a day's time. At the slower pace, it took approximately 15-20 days to cross the Atlantic Ocean. Dad was fortunate that none of the ships he sailed on were ever attacked by airplanes or submarines. Eventually tragedy would find them in another way.

Civilians manned the privately owned ships and were not part of the armed forces. Dad made 14 trips on 7 different Liberty ships across the Atlantic to Europe and back. Of course the enemy did everything they could to keep the ships carrying supplies from landing at their port. Most that sank were due to submarine fire.

Seas could be high and storms rough enough to cause sea sickness. Dad didn't get physically sick but would just feel bad. Some had a harder time with seasickness than others. During his tours as a seaman his destinations were primarily England, and, Italy and Sicily through the Mediterranean Sea.

Typically Dad was a fireman, stoker or water tender, in the engine room. There were two boilers, each having 4 burners, which had to be cleaned every 8 hours. Dad kept the fire going and the temperature where it needed to be. On his most notable 14th and final trip abroad he was an oiler keeping the pistons and crankshaft oiled. There was a platform above to place the oil which ran down a tube to keep them lubricated.

CHAPTER 11

THE PORT OF ANTWERP

A memorable cruise for Dad was carrying supplies to Antwerp, Belgium. In June 1944, after the success of D-Day in Normandy, France, the Antwerp shipping port became vital to the Allies receiving supplies. In September 1944, British forces captured the city of Antwerp with its port intact. Since the breakout from Normandy, the front line had moved northward at an astonishing pace. (4) Supplies were desperately needed. The ship Dad was on was destined to Antwerp through the English Channel and 45 miles up the river Scheldt.

There were several hundred ships waiting in line to deliver at the port. This was one of the only times Dad recalled delivering PX supplies instead of trucks, tanks, and ammunition. PX was a Post Exchange where the servicemen bought their necessities, like you and I might buy at our local Target store or grocer. Because PX supplies were not the highest priority at the time, the ship Dad was on waited in the harbor 20 days for their turn to unload.

In the meantime, the Germans were trying to thwart the Allies' efforts by sending "buzz bombs" into Antwerp approximately every 20 minutes. The Germans had first focused their "buzz bombs" on the city of London prior to D-Day. Once they saw the Allies gaining ground they focused the "buzz bombs" on Antwerp and its port.

A "buzz bomb" resembled a small airplane with short, stubby wings. It was propelled by a simple jet engine with a limited range of 148 miles. Dad said they sounded like an old truck without a muffler. At night they would hear the erratic sound of the motor. Then it would shut off and there would be silence while they waited for it to land and explode, hoping it would not come down over them. The bombs were plentiful but the Germans had not perfected them. Their aim was only as good as the amount of gas in the motor. When the gas ran out the bomb would either glide until it hit something or would drop straight down and explode. The day had finally arrived for Dad's ship to unload. As they were only one ship away from the dock to unload, a bomb hit the dock and killed a military policeman. The Allies were not allowed to shoot down the bombs because that might cause them to fall on the port.

The last day Dad was in Antwerp the men were allowed to disembark for a few hours. They could not pass their time at the movie theater as it had been bombed a few days before killing several people. They enjoyed just being off the ship and having free time to roam the city.

During the same time, the Battle of the Bulge was happening nearby. Even more the reason the supply ships were needed. German forces had launched a surprise attack on Allied Forces in the forested Ardennes region in Belgium, Luxembourg, and France. After a month the Allied counter offensive forced German troops to withdraw.(5)

CHAPTER 12

THE FINAL VOYAGE

On the previously mentioned 14th and final trip to Europe as a merchant seaman, the ship Dad was on stopped in Sicily, unloaded and returned north to Civitavecchia, Italy. They anchored in the bay with lots of other ships just as a bad storm was brewing. The anchor would not hold so there was no choice but to go out to sea, cruise around and wait out the storm.

The following morning just before daylight, Dad was in his bunk asleep when he heard the engines start. He got out of bed and was putting his clothes on when the ship hit a mine. He left his bunk room going topside and saw a life raft on a 45 degree angle. He witnessed the chief cook pull the release on the raft, then jump overboard and abandon ship without authorization. No one was sure if he made it into the raft but he was never seen again.

They examined the hole the mine had created and determined it was not too severe so they continued on. Approximately an hour later, the ship hit two mines that were tied together. Approximately one third or more of the front of the ship was gone. They soon abandoned ship and got into lifeboats. The ship was equipped with four lifeboats, which accommodated 18 people each, and four life rafts. Attempts to lower lifeboats on the port side were unsuccessful because of high waves and wind, so they lowered them on the starboard side.

Everyone entered the lifeboats as the storm was heavily upon them. Among them was a woman that the Captain had brought aboard, which according to regulations was an unauthorized passenger and not allowed.

They rode out the rough seas in the midst of the cold and winter morning for about four hours. With the wind blowing them toward shore, the closer they got to the shore the worse the waves were. The tall waves were well above them crashing into the lifeboat and filling it with water. Steadily pumping the handle on the bilge pump was fruitless. The rain and waves were filling the boat with water. The waves continuously threw them out of the lifeboat eventually capsizing it. They would swim back to it and hold on or try to climb back on over and over and over again. While the fight to stay with the lifeboat continued another two hours, everyone was seasick and growing tired from fighting the waves. If not for the life vests, no one would have survived.

After seeing land on the horizon and the wind blowing toward the shore, Dad chose to leave the others and swim to shore. Local sheepherders on horseback arrived at the shore at the same time Dad did. They spotted him and helped him onto the beach. Eventually, others from the crew appeared near the beach, all in a weakened state and were dragged ashore. The Captain and his lady friend survived. She was found further down the beach where she had ridden the broken mast from the lifeboat to shore. Everyone from the lifeboats eventually made it ashore, all 40+ of them. Sadly, however, there were two casualties. Assuming the Cook was dead, he was the first. The second was an older man that stayed drunk a lot. He had lost two boys in the war and was grieving. He drank whisky every chance he got. So sad the impact of war.

There was a man from Michigan, who was a little older than Dad, in his life boat. He later wrote Dad a letter thanking him for saving his life during the storm. He also visited Dad decades later and again thanked him as he knew he wouldn't be here today if not for Dad's help. Dad said he was just helping those he could.

CHAPTER 13

RECOVERY

It was December 29, 1945 and the weather was very cold. The sheep-herders took the survivors to a barn and made a fire out of hay to help dry them. They were then carried to a local hotel where they were served drinks to warm them up. Dad usually did not partake in alcohol, but said he may have that day! The survivors stayed at the hotel about four hours, but did not sleep there since the War Ship Administration had been noti-fied. An open air truck had been ordered to pick them up and take them to Rome. It was a cold ride.

In Rome the survivors stayed in the hospital for 3-4 days and were issued Army uniforms to have something clean and dry to wear. After their hospital stay they convalesced for a week at Mussolini's Palace. Mussolini had already been overthrown and killed fleeing from Italy to Switzerland. The palace had a big swimming pool and of course the famous balcony where Mussolini gave his speeches. Even though Dad was not injured it was a nice place to rest after such an experience.

During the daytime, those that were physically able took in the sites of Rome. Dad did not talk about these days as we were growing up. It wasn't until my family and I visited Europe in 2013 and came home tell-ing Mom and Dad about our trip to Rome that pieces of his experience began emerging. He asked, "did you go up into the dome while visiting St. Peter's Basilica?" He said they had and the story began its revelation.

After leaving Rome they were taken south by truck to Naples. There they boarded a ship to go home. For the first time Dad was a passenger on a Liberty ship. Bunks about 4-5 high were placed in the cargo hole for them. They passed the time by shooting dice, playing poker and sitting on deck watching the sea.

Upon arriving home an officer questioned every merchant seaman on the mined ship. What happened, what did you see, how did you survive? Dad was asked to name all the people on his life boat. He named all but one. Once he did, he was told to go ahead and name the 'other one'. None of the seamen had mentioned the woman on board, but the officer already knew. When asked, Dad confirmed the woman was onboard.

The bombed ship never sank entirely. During their stay in Rome, a group of the seamen were preparing to salvage the ship and claim salvage rights. The War Administration halted the recovery efforts.

CHAPTER 14

THE WAR IS ENDING

After his last European voyage, Dad made one last trip with the Merchant Marines, which was up the eastern seaboard to Nova Scotia. They never left the ship during this sailing. In Nova Scotia the ship was loaded with lead ore. The temperature was cold and they were cautioned to be aware of icebergs. With the war being over and the ammunition on board not needed, they utilized the icebergs to dispose of their leftover ammunition by shooting into them. The remainder was dumped at sea.

After the ship was loaded they were leaving the inlet and ran aground. A tugboat was sent to help. The tug hooked on to the aft trying all night to pull the ship off land. Since the efforts to free them, up to this point, were unsuccessful the seamen set to work unloading the number one hole of lead ore. Using winches it was hoisted and dumped overboard. The ship finally came loose. The lead ore stayed behind in the water.

To check out the possible damage to the ship's hull from the grounding, their next stop was St. John's Harbor in Nova Scotia. Divers were sent to look underneath the ship to inspect the damage. There was damage and a risk but they were okayed to continue on. While in the harbor they saw two German submarines who had received word the war was over and had surrendered. Dad's ship received orders to continue their journey to Houston, Texas to deliver their load. They traveled around Miami, up the channel past Galveston to the Port of Houston. The ship would stay in port to repair damages. Dad took a train from Houston to Nahunta and his sailing days were over.

In 2002 my sister, Jaren, toured a visiting Liberty ship in Brunswick, Georgia with Mom and Dad. Dad showed them where he worked in the engine room and where the ship broke in two when the second mine hit. It was an emotional event for him to relive.

CHAPTER 15

HOME TO STAY?

After Dad completed his last trip with the Merchant Marines he quit and went to work for his Dad in his ice business. This was in the mid 1940s when there were only iceboxes and no refrigerators. They purchased blocks of ice from the icehouse in Waycross to stock their own ice business in Nahunta.

Papa's ice house was located on Main Street between Campbell's Drug Store and today's police station. It was a busy place on Friday and Saturday. People wanted ice tea for the weekend!

Dad drove the ice delivery truck, a wooden 1935 Ford with no doors or brakes! He would load blocks of ice on an open bed covered with a tarp to start his deliveries. One night he was two miles outside of Nahunta after dark when the truck lights went out. He could only see the lines on the road by leaning out of the truck. Once he got to his destination he stepped out but the truck had not stopped. He hit the ground, rolled, got up and chased after the truck. After successfully catching the truck, Dad made his delivery. However, his employment in the ice business was very short lived.

CHAPTER 16

YOU'RE IN THE ARMY NOW

The war had ended but the war time draft was still in effect. The draft did not apply to those in the Merchant Marines, but having recently ended that stint, Dad received his draft notice. Thirty-six men from Brantley County received draft notices. Dad and John Davis were the only two that passed the test. The others failed and had also been turned down before. After all the risks and time spent in the Merchant Marines, Dad would now officially serve his country in the Army in the very last war time draft of World War II.

Dad had only been home from the Merchant Marines for a short time. Thinking he was home for good, he soon realized he would be shipping out again. He took a train to Fort Bragg, North Carolina for 6 weeks of basic training. He went back home for a few days and prepared for his trip abroad. Getting across the U.S.A. in the 1940s wasn't as easy as it is today. He first took a train to Jacksonville where he boarded a plane to New Orleans. This is the only time in his life he has ever flown in an airplane. Next, he took a train to Los Angeles and another train to San Francisco. They handed out blankets on the train to San Francisco, which puzzled him as it was summertime. He figured it out quickly when they got off the train in San Francisco and it was cold. He was soon on a ship to Japan. Even after all of his cruises to Europe, this was uncharted territory for him.

CHAPTER 17

JAPAN

Many servicemen were being sent home as the war was winding down. However, the final draft provided men to help in the transition. Dad was stationed in Yokohama in the 8th Army Headquarters Division motor pool. He drove a Jeep taking American civilian businessmen to work in the War Shipping Administration for the government. Most were going to the main office building in Tokyo, which was approximately 17 miles from Yokohama. One day Dad had just dropped off the men when he saw guards outside the building preparing for something which piqued his interest, so he kept watching. Soon he saw General Douglas MacArthur come out of the building, get into a vehicle and was chauffeured away.

While in the Army Dad began participating in competitive boxing. Since he was representing the Army during his fights and to further support his boxing efforts, Dad's work assignment was changed. Instead of driving the American businessmen to Tokyo, he was assigned to drive children of American military families to school. He would pick up 2-3 children who lived up the mountain where the school bus could not go. While they were in school he picked up the mail, worked out at the school's gym and played basketball to maintain his conditioning to stay in top form for his boxing matches. When school was over, he took the children home.

There were clubs in Yokohama that sponsored boxing matches where Dad would sign up. He occasionally had a trainer that would assist him in the ring. Dad weighed 183 lbs and you had to be over 175 lbs to qualify for heavyweight fights. During his year of stay in Japan he consistently held the heavyweight boxing champion title for three of Japan's primary islands, Honshu, Kyushu and Okinawa.

Once on his day off, Dad was able to meet up with his younger brother Joe where he was stationed at a large naval base in Negishi near Yokohama. This is where the infamous monkey picture that I had seen over the years originated. Dad has a picture of him, Uncle Joe and a monkey, which is sitting on Uncle Joe's head. A man gave the monkey to Dad, which he kept around the barracks. He left him behind for others to care for once he was sent home.

After spending approximately 18 months in the army and the draft discontinued, the army converted to strictly accepting volunteers. Those that were still under the draft could go home or volunteer for four more years. It was an easy choice for dad - goodbye Army, hello Nahunta. Most boys who had served were already home. Dad's penned memories which are documented in the Epologue stated, "Not all made it back. I pray they are in Heaven."

Dad was sent home from Japan and was officially out of the Army. He took a year off as jobs were scarce. Veterans were drawing $21 a month from the government if you couldn't find a job. It was required to report monthly on your job search. You had to name four places you had applied for a job to continue to receive the money. Wanting to take some time off, Dad was not actively searching for a job, so he only received the payment one month. He was back living at home and had no transportation.

CHAPTER 18

FIRST CAME LOVE

Dad first met Mom when she was 15 and he was 20 years old. Dad's memories printed in the Epilogue said mom was "the most beautiful, wonderful girl in the world". After being married to mom for 58 years he wrote "and the above description of her still stands".

Mom was living with her aunt and uncle, Jewell and Albert Purdom while she attended Nahunta High School. One evening Mom, Julia Blanche Grimes to others, had gone with four other girls to The Sweet Shop on Main Street. It had a soda fountain where people could hang out and drink a float, shake or have a snack. There was a Halloween carnival going on just outside town in Hickox at the old school. They all wanted to go but had no ride. They decided that the next young, single man with a car that walked through the door, they would ask for a ride to the carnival. The young, single and good looking guy was Dad along with his friend Joe Smith, who owned the car. They piled into the car, Mom in the backseat. They all enjoyed the carnival and when it was time to head back to town, Mom was about to enter the backseat again when Dad motioned for her to get in the front seat by him….and the love story began.

Mom played varsity basketball at Nahunta High School. Dad loved basketball and began attending some of the games. One night she was on the court but not feeling well. She motioned several times to the coach to take her out of the game but it never happened. She soon fainted on the court. Dad ran down the bleachers to see about her and subsequently drove her home. She remembered telling Aunt Jewell the next day, "you are never going to believe who brought me home last night". That was the beginning of a four year courtship. Dad recalls that their favorite song while dating was "My Happiness" by Connie Francis.

When Dad came home from the war, he still found time for the sports he loved so much. In addition to boxing and basketball, baseball was his other passion. He played on an Arco sponsored team. Arco is a community on the western outskirts of Brunswick. Dad played short-stop and third base. He must have been good as during my life I have had people tell me they loved to watch him play. At one point he and his buddy, Claude Smith, worked out in Jesup, Georgia with a professional team. Dad received an offer to play in the minor leagues but took a job at Hercules in Brunswick instead as he and Mom were about to be married. Minor league professional teams did not pay well enough to feed a family.

Dad and Mom were married December 30, 1949 by the pastor of the First Baptist Church in Nahunta. Mom had some of her girlfriends in attendance and Dad had his best friend, Claude Smith, as his best man. For their honeymoon they drove south to the Florida-Georgia line but the large motel had no vacancy. They ate a meal there and kept going to Hilliard where there was a rooming house. Men employed by the power company had just left that day which created a vacancy for them. The next day they drove to Jacksonville and on to Brunswick for Dad to go to work the following day.

Mom and Dad lived with her Aunt Dora Stephens in Brunswick. Dad had purchased a 1948 Chevy with 11,000 miles. He was employed by Hercules. Hercules refined products from pine stumps. In 1948, the year prior to his employment, they began making a pesticide called Toxaphene. Dad worked in the chemical department putting bags of lime in a vat of chlorine used in making Toxaphene. The lime would neutralize the chlorine so that it could be run into the Brunswick River as waste. Unfortunately, there were no safety precautions for the employees who were working around this chemical. It is believed that Dad became a severe asthmatic at the age of 24 due to the lack of these safety precautions.

CHAPTER 19

THEN THE BABY CARRIAGE

Marie Lynette Jones was born January 9, 1951 while Dad was working at Hercules. One day Dad was taking care of Lynette while Mom was at work. Mom's Aunt Gertie Lynn was visiting and told the story she thought was so funny seeing Dad up on the bed on his knees trying to change a diaper. He got the job done regardless of his unorthodox method. Three years later, I, Jana Laverne Jones, was born February 5, 1954.

After a few years Dad quit the Hercules to move back to his beloved hometown of Nahunta. This put them closer to family, friends, hunting and fishing.

When we moved to Nahunta we lived in Dad's old home place which Papa had built. It was across the small road from the Brantley Telephone Company. Papa lived upstairs while Mom, Dad, Lynette and I lived downstairs.

Dad took a job at the REA (Rural Electric Authority) as Foreman of the right-away crew cutting trees and bushes away from the lines. Later there was a problem with an employee not getting along with some of the pole climbers so they switched Dad to climbing poles so they could move the other employee to Foreman of the right away crew. Dad had great physical strength to climb poles but his asthma was taking a toll.

The exertion was aggravating his breathing. It soon became apparent he would be unable to continue in this job.

In 1956 when Dad left the REA, he took a job as Brantley County Sheriff's Deputy. The Sheriff was ex-GBI agent Earl Raulerson and his office was located in the Court House. We then moved a few blocks to the center of town, living in the jailhouse. Dad's job was to lock up the bad guys while Mom's was to feed the prisoners. Mom and Dad were reimbursed $1.20 per meal for serving the prisoners. She provided the prisoners two meals a day. The jailhouse was a two story brick building. Our home was on the first floor and the prisoners were on the second floor. To access their food, the prisoners had a stairway within their confines that descended to a roll up window in our kitchen. It was kept locked except when Mom was passing their meals through it.

As Deputy Sheriff, Dad did not carry a gun. The Sheriff's Office did not have any guns to issue to the deputies. If you owned a gun, you could carry it. Dad had a 22 rifle under the front seat of his patrol car, but did not have one to carry on him. Later, a gun was taken off a prisoner. Once released, he didn't request it be returned to him so Dad kept it in his glove box.

Dad was paid $150 a month, plus $5 per arrest that was adjudicated by the court. He drove his own 1955 Chevrolet that had "County Police" painted on the side and was provided a badge. He paid for his gas and wore civilian clothes.

One day Dad received a call from the Jesup, Georgia authorities. They were looking for an escaped prisoner and he was believed to be headed south toward Nahunta. Dad found the escapee's vehicle wrecked into a tree north of Nahunta. It was abandoned and the escapee was nowhere in sight. Dad and others started searching the woods in the area where the car was found. Unbeknownst to them, the escapee had headed to Nahunta jailhouse to break out his friend named Dink. Mom was at home with Lynette and I, who were very young at the time. Mom heard the escapee outside the jailhouse calling for Dink and saying he was going to blow up the jail. The Sheriff's cars had no radios, so Mom called the Georgia Highway Patrol to get word to Dad. Her fear was that the escapee may come into our house in search of guns or maybe even blow up the jail, which we lived in. They never found the escapee and assumed he jumped on a train that had recently come through Nahunta. He was not successful in getting his friend Dink out of jail.

After living two years in the jailhouse, Dad ran for Sheriff against the incumbent Mr. Earl Raulerson and Mr. Crews. Mr. Crews won. Dad quit the Sheriff's Department. We moved out of the jailhouse and back to Dad's old home place with Papa living upstairs.

The old garage was still beside the house where Dad had played basketball as a kid. In the backyard we had a sandbox where I contracted ringworms in my foot. My parents used a freezing product to freeze my foot which killed the ringworms - not a pleasant experience. There were plenty of woods next to the house to create trails and small clearings for club meetings with our friends. There was a long clothes line in the backyard to hang wet laundry to dry. If we could not reach the line to hang clothes, we helped Mom by handing clothes and pins. We had great neighbors. The Riggins girls, Linda, Gail, Sandra and Vicky, lived behind us. Mary Beth Lloyd lived down the street. They would join us to play as well as other friends from town did. When we were young we made our own fun. That may mean you need to dig around in the garbage for cans and look for a long sturdy stick. Then you have all the makings of the game Knock the Tin Cans.

Across Highway 82 from our house lived Lena and Avery Strickland and their children. When Lynette was ten and I was seven, Mom was about to have another baby. While she was in the hospital, we stayed at their home for a night or two. I was so excited. They lived in a long, nice, brick house and had real lace up roller skates we could use to skate on their driveway. Little things mean a lot when you are young.

Jaren Orr Jones was born October 14, 1960. Mom had complications with the delivery. Mom and Jaren came home from the hospital but Mom soon had to return due to the complications. Dad managed the Bay Station on the north side of town and had to work during the day, so Lynette and I were left in charge of the newborn. Again, we were 10 and 7 years old at that time. Things were really different in those days! Aunt Jewell told a story about how she came over to check on us one day. We were preparing a meal. Jaren was in her bassinet. Lynette had pulled a chair over to the stove so I could stand in it to stir a pot. Mom said she laid in the hospital and cried many tears as she felt helpless not being there with us.

Just as Dad's family did at Christmas, we all loaded up in the car and Mom and Dad would take us into the woods to chop down our tree. Looking back, it looked much like a Charlie Brown Christmas tree but to us it was beautiful. We got some gifts from Santa Claus and our parents but it was always special when our great Aunt June and great Uncle Wes visited from Florida and brought us Christmas presents. It was always a special gift and we looked forward to them each year.

One holiday we did not celebrate was Halloween. Dad was not in favor of us going house to house trick-or-treating for candy as it seemed like begging. We were okay handing out candy from home and maybe saving a few pieces for ourselves.

Dad managed the gas station just north of town on Highway 301. The station's name changed three times while he managed it. First it was the Speed Station, then the Bay Station and lastly the Tenneco Station. He sold tires and batteries as well as fuel. Highway 301 was the main traffic route on the east coast as I-95 had not been built. Many large trucks stopped for diesel fuel and snacks. Dad didn't have any boys to help him so he used girl power. Mom would read the fuel pumps and balance the register at the end of each day. When Lynette was old enough, Mom taught her. Lynette and I would be dispatched to pick up trash around the property and load the drink machine. J R Patton worked for Dad during this time. I remember J R pushing us around the station in a little white car. The car was not a toy but was extremely small for a road car. The door opened from the front of the car. Lots of fun! I am not sure how the little car was acquired, but he was known to accept trade from desperate travelers who had no money. He provided gas, tires, or a battery for trade. He received watches, a pop-up camper and other miscellaneous things. That pop-up camper provided us with a few vacations over the years.

Dad was the disciplinarian. He worked most weekends so when we got home from church, and he joined us for lunch, he would ask if any of us acted up during church. If Mom named one of us, you would go straight to the bathroom, missing lunch and await your punishment, which was usually his belt. He certainly took the scripture of Proverbs 13:24 regarding "Spare the rod, spoil the child" seriously.

Lynette and I had a few battles growing up which is typical for siblings close in age. Once I complained to Dad that Lynette did something to me. He asked what I wanted him to do about it. I said, "spank her". He told me to get the belt for him and when I did he used it on me for tattling. Lesson learned. That man didn't play!

Mom always took us to church every Sunday. We went to the First Baptist Church where she taught Sunday School. One Sunday in the early 1960s, I was upstairs in Sunday School when one of the mother's of a student came in and abruptly asked for her child. No one knew why and she didn't say. Afterwards an alarm went off and we were escorted outside and advised there was a gas leak in the building. After a while we were given the all clear and told church service would be held as planned. During church we began seeing people get up and leave and a person slumped on to the pew. The gas leak was not corrected and we were all evacuated. After we got home, Mom was in bed terribly sick. Us girls weren't feeling great either. We called Dad and told him what had happened at church. Very soon he came barreling over the front sidewalk in the car to the front steps. He didn't use the driveway but the closest entry to the house and to Mom. He picked up Mom, got us kids in the car and took off a short way down the road to the doctor's office. Apparently many had been affected as the place was crowded with church members. Mom was eventually okay but it was a scare for sure.

For entertainment Mom and Dad joined other couples in town for square dancing. The town doctor organized the events. Square dancing is something you rarely hear of any more. Mom would wear her shin length, very full skirt with crinolines under it. I still have one of Mom's skirts that my granddaughter, Ashley, wore to high school for '50's day'. Dad dressed in a buttoned up shirt with his bolo tie. What a sight that was watching them have fun!

Business at Dad's station was good enough to make a living, but once I-95 was built on the east coast, traffic on Highway 301 began dwindling. Dad's Uncle Wes and Aunt June, who lived in Belle Glade, Florida, told him of a gas station in the middle of town called McMillans that needed management. Dad took a trip to Belle Glade, assessed the opportunity and accepted it. He moved to Belle Glade in early 1965 and lived with Aunt June and Uncle Wes for several months until he purchased a house on S.E. 2nd Street. Mom and us kids stayed in Nahunta until school was out and then moved down in June of 1965. Papa stayed in Nahunta.

CHAPTER 20

FLORIDA

Lynette had completed eighth grade, I had completed fifth grade and Jaren was five years old when we moved to Belle Glade. This move was especially hard for Lynette because she was older and didn't like leaving behind her friends. I missed my friends too, but Jaren and I were at a more adaptable age. We all went on to make lifelong friends in Belle Glade. We have great friends in both Florida and Georgia.

Dad was a very hard working man. However, his love for baseball never waned. For several years he coached a women's city league softball team in Belle Glade with Mom playing first base and me roving fielder. We came in first place several years. Dad was a great coach. The ladies loved him. I will say being the coach's daughter came with a bit more instruction, as I went home with him after the games. There were times I would have to run laps or maybe spend time practicing "stepping into that swing". After all, it was for my own development. That's just difficult to see as a teenager.

Dad still had the love for hunting and fishing. He would leave Mom in charge of his business for a few days to return to Nahunta when hunting and fishing was at its best. One trip he headed out and Mom realized he had not left the ring of keys for the business. She quickly loaded us girls into the car and was trying to catch up with him when the police stopped her for speeding. Jaren was very young and crying in the backseat, worried that Mom was going to jail. The compassion-ate policeman radioed the Florida Highway Patrol to stop Dad. They did and all was well when Dad turned around and took Mom the keys. Fortunately, Mom's perfect record of having no wrecks and receiving no tickets in all her years of driving was not blemished.

Dad also had a boat in Belle Glade for bass fishing and one large enough we could water ski in the rim canal of Lake Okeechobee. Unfortunately, Dad worked a lot and I remember the boat being in our driveway much more than in the water.

Over time the McMillan Station was torn down. Dad moved his gas, tire and battery business to another location near the airport. The thing that stands out most about this station was Dad's require-ments for us to help out. We were unpaid help but we did learn re-sponsibility. So the girl power was reimplemented. Actually it never stopped. We helped Dad on occasion but we also helped Mom at the house. One of our responsibilities at the station, which was called City Tire & Gas Service, was to fuel automobiles, clean their wind-shield and collect the money. Of course this was before self-serve pumps. It was particularly awkward when one of our friends or the popular guys from school came in. Lynette and I would sit on the bench out front playing a form of 'Let's Make a Deal' of who knew them best and begging the other one to serve this customer. Teens are easily embarrassed! Little Jaren also got in on the action by filling the cigarette machine.

During our dating years Dad was still very much in control. Any major event such as a date, party, dance, or sleepover with our girl-friends had to have his approval after getting Mom's. He would not commit in advance. It was usually the night before or day of the event before we got the green light. As a parent, I now understand his con-cerns especially since there was a 30 foot deep canal beside the road to West Palm Beach, which is where some dates took place.

Eventually Dad's business moved from the gas station at Airport Road to an old Budweiser Beer warehouse he purchased and turned into a tire warehouse where he could perform front end alignments. It was called Jones Tire & Battery. There was no gas to pump anymore. Mom helped in the office. When a semi truck full of tires was scheduled to arrive it was all hands on deck. In the warehouse there were aisles with tires stored floor to ceiling on racks, based on tire size. Tires had to be removed from the semi on a timely basis, the tire size on the tire read, and the tire rolled to the appropriate aisle, which would later be put onto the tire racks. It was hard work, but looking back on our work experiences, it made us conscientious workers for life.

While Dad had the tire warehouse, there was a man who did mechanic work on cars just on the other side of the fence. He and Dad talked over the fence regularly. When the man had some serious health problems and wasn't able to work for a while, Dad took him money to help him get by. Dad liked placing his help for others directly in the hands of those in need, which I know he did many times in his life.

In January 1972, Dad received a call that Papa had been rushed to the hospital in Waycross, Georgia which is about 25 miles west of Nahunta. Lynette was in college in Jacksonville at the time, so she went to Waycross as Dad was driving up from Belle Glade. Unfortunately, Papa died of an abdominal aortic aneurysm before they arrived. He was 80 years old. Subsequently, both of Dad's brothers died; Joe from colon cancer in 1990 and Sibert from an auto accident in 1996. Dad's parents and siblings had all passed on.

During the 15 or so years Mom and Dad lived in Belle Glade, Dad continued to suffer with his asthma. He would catch a simple cold and end up in the hospital in intensive care hardly able to breathe. Once we took him to the VA Hospital in Lake City. He was told he had lung cancer. Eventually, it was determined it was a misdiagnosis. While at the VA on a different visit he was being discharged and had left a piece of paper on the side table. The paper read: "I've never fired a shot, but you treated me like I won the war." He was always concerned about taking advantage of his VA benefits. Because he had only spent about 18 months in the Army during the last wartime draft, Dad in some way felt he wasn't deserving to accept those benefits. However, being self-employed, we had no health insurance so at times it was needed and appreciated.

CHAPTER 21

BACK TO GEORGIA

In 1980, Mom and Dad moved back to Nahunta. He managed another gas station for a short time and then opened up a small tire store on the property beside the old home place. By then, us girls were on our own. I remember buying my first house in Jacksonville and making a loan agreement with Dad for the down payment. He showed up with $7,000 in cash in a brown paper bag - true Ben Jones style.

In 1983, Mom and Dad were desperately seeking improvement for Dad's breathing. They heard the drier weather in Arizona may help so they drove to Phoenix, Arizona and rented a small apartment for 6-8 weeks. Mom's brother, Sammy, lived in Phoenix. He took Mom sightseeing to the Grand Canyon, but Dad was unable to go. They went home after Dad was hospitalized a couple of times, receiving no positive results with his breathing.

Dad loved "his girls" as he would call us. That always included my mother as well. Two days before Thanksgiving in 1984, Mom found a piece of paper where Dad had written down the things he was thankful for.

THANKS

-for the many blessings I see each day
-for my girls and theirs

-for the balance that keeps this mind in a positive setting
-for those that have offered my name for consideration in
their relationship with God
-for those that traveled life's road here on earth before me
and the good things I share because of them
-for prayer, thru which we may ask God that our sins be
forgiven
-for acknowledging Jesus Christ as our only source for a
continued life after death
-for knowledge to eradicate misery on this earth as God
would have us do

As we married the grandchildren began arriving. In 1981 my son, Ben Bramlett, was born first and was named after his grandfather who he named Poppy. Mom and I spoke frequently by phone. She was anxiously awaiting the birth and to become a grandmother. She was ready to go to Jacksonville to help after the baby was born. When my water broke and we were on the way to the hospital, I called and spoke to Dad. Mom was not at home so I told him to tell her. The next day I had not heard from her so I called to report the birth and gender. Since there were no routine sonograms back then, the gender was a surprise. Mom was excited and shocked I had delivered the baby. I asked, "Didn't Dad tell you I called yesterday?" Later, he said he didn't want to worry her and she would want to go to Jacksonville before it was time.

Next came Lynette's two children, Andrew and Morgan Thompson, and then Jaren's two children, Jake and Jacy Robertson. All total Mom and Dad have 3 daughters, 5 grandchildren and 6 great grandchildren. The great grandchildren are Ashley, Lauren, Lisa, Leah (Ben), Wesley (Andrew), and Thompson (Morgan).

In 1999 for Fathers Day I wrote this poem which sums up well my feelings for Dad.

IN MY EYES

It's hard to describe how much it means to have a father like you
It's clear that a mere thanks would never do
The respect I have for you
Far exceeds any I ever knew

When I was but a little one
I knew then what God had done
He'd placed me in a loving home
With a leader that was well known

A king, a prince, a president he was not
But in my eyes he carried a bigger lot
A giant of sorts
Who loved his sports

A coach to me
When I was not all I could be
A mentor when I needed advice
To a little girl he was bigger than life

Respect, honesty and love are his virtues
I knew then no one could fill his shoes
Now I have grown up, but nothing has changed
Your love is constant and treatment the same

I needed a name for my only child
It didn't take much thought or a list to compile
I knew that my hero was my Dad
So Ben's the name his grandson has

Dad, while our life is quickly passing
Please always know my love for you is everlasting

THE GOLDEN YEARS

In 1988 when Dad decided to retire, he bought land a few miles east of Nahunta where they have lived for 32 years. When he was 15 years old, George Dykes interested him in fox hunting and that has never waned. Dad fenced his land and stocked it with fox and coyotes. He has had upward to 35 dogs at one time. He would breed them and train them to hunt the fox and coyotes. He would take his best dogs to field trials in north Florida and up through central Georgia for competitions. Eventually he was on trophy overload. He no longer travels to competitions today, but still enjoys the sport on his own land with fewer dogs.

Dad was never one for giving gifts nor one to remember holidays, but he would pen his thoughts from time to time. This is a letter he wrote to my Mom for Valentine's Day in 1995, which is framed and hanging in their home.

My Sweet,

On this Sweetheart day I am reminded of the many things that keep me in love with you.

You just being you, the dishes and clothes you wash, the house you keep, the way you used to jump up at night when the babies would cry. The steps you make for me, the mother you are and have been to our three girls and many other things. I denote a little love in all the above. Blanche your happiness means an awful lot to me. I know my love for you is at an all-time high. These 46 years have passed in a hurry, but because of you they have all been great.

Blanche I respect you, I love you and want you to continue to be my Valentine.

Love
Ben

Dad's health issues continued. In the early 1990s his heart went into atrial fibrillation. After a couple of unsuccessful attempts to correct it, he has lived with AFIB for over 30 years. He survived prostate cancer in 1996 after receiving pinpoint radiation seeding, which at the time was only available in Seattle and Atlanta. Fortunately, Jaren lived near Atlanta at the time so he stayed with her during the treatment. In 2014 he had upward to 50 kidney stones at one time, some of which were very difficult to pass and one bout that put him in intensive care with sepsis. Over the years modern medicine would provide improvement for his asthma, but nothing better than the success he found in 2017 after visiting Mayo Clinic in Jacksonville. He began taking an asthma drug, which gave him a new life. He also began receiving an injection every eight weeks to help his lungs.

In October 2020, at the age of 94, Dad tested positive for Covid-19. He felt really bad for about 3 weeks and had a fever for 13 consecutive days. This took place while he was taking care of our 89 year old Mom, who got sick two days after he did. What a helpless feeling as us girls made deliveries to their doorstep of food and routine medications and talked to them from the yard while they sat on the porch, if they were able to leave the bed. During one visit we were going over the food options that Dad could make. He said he didn't even feel like opening a can. Dad had lost 20 pounds. At one point Jaren had the EMTs go to their house to check them out. Another visit Jaren took them a banana split and he enjoyed it so much we knew he was turning the corner and Mom was better by then as well. They were never hospitalized and fully recovered. Thank you Lord!

Dad is now 95 and Mom is 90 years old and they have been together 75 years - married 71 years plus the 4 years they dated! They still live alone on their land in the country with no assistance other than intermittently from us girls. Dad is still managing his dogs. With a new litter of puppies he has about 12 total. He still mows the yard, uses his tractor to mow parts of the fox pen, uses a chainsaw which at this writing is stuck in a tree, and maintains the fencing and electric wiring for his hunting pen.

Dad is certainly an inspiration. He hurts a lot, walks slowly and unsteady due to neuropathy in his feet and sleep often eludes him. He never gives up no matter what. For example, after a lot of rain in early 2021, debris from the woods was blocking a culvert where his property meets the paved road. He and Mom took the all-terrain cart and parked beside the road at the culvert. Dad tied a rope to the cart and the other end around his chest and lowered himself into the swamp to clean away the debris. He then pulled himself out with his arms and the rope. My goodness, I am glad we hear about these things after the fact! A few years ago sitting on his back porch in his swing, he told me he felt the Lord had left him on earth so long to take care of Mom.

What an interesting, full life this man has lived. We are blessed to have such wonderful parents and cherish our days with them!

PHOTOGRAPHS

Benjamin Franklin Jones and wife Melissa

Dr. Jerome Orr, wife Ida, and children Flossie and Calvin

Flossie and Dan Jones on their wedding day in Hoboken, Ga on March 12, 1918

Top hat worn by the men in the Orr family. Labels shows it was made in Paris.

Flossie Orr Jones with her first two sons – Sibert 3 years old and
Ben 5 months and 3 weeks weighing 17 ¾ lbs. July 1926

Ben Jones as a toddler in 1927

17 year old Ben Jones in a Navy uniform while in Merchant Marine training. 1943

Mussolini's Palace in Rome, with the famous balcony,
where the seamen convalesced in early January 1946

Ben Jones in the Army in Japan. 1946

*Joe and Ben Jones and the infamous monkey,
seen on Joe's head, in Negishi, Japan. 1946*

Ben Jones in uniform for the Arco baseball team. 1950s

Ben Jones, top left player, on the Hercules basketball team.

The brothers...L-R Sibert, Joe, Ben in Okeechobee, Florida Christmas of 1956

Lynette, Jaren and Jana Jones in front of the old home place in the early 1960s

Lynette and Michael Thompson with children Andrew and Morgan

Jana and Ed Woodall with son Ben and granddaughter Ashley

Jaren and W.S. Robertson with children Jake and Jacy

Ben Jones introducing his grandson, Ben, to one of his puppies. 1982

Blanche and Ben Jones headed to a luau. 1998

Ben Jones feeding his many dogs

Ben Jones with the one that DID NOT get away - a 11 1/2 lb bass. 1977

Blanche and Ben Jones

The Ben and Blanche Jones family Christmas 2007.
L-R...Michael, Andrew, Lynette, Morgan, Jaren, Jake,
Ben, Jacy, Ashley, W.S., Jana, Ed, Blanche, Ben

Waycross Journal-Herald, Monday, February 14, 2000

Mr. And Mrs. Ben Jones
Celebrate 50th Anniversary

NAHUNTA — Mr. and Mrs. Ben O. Jones of Nahunta celebrated their 50th wedding anniversary on Dec. 30, 1999 with a reception held in their honor on St. Simons Island. Their three daughters, Lynette (Mrs. Michael) Thompson and Jana (Mrs. Edward) Woodall, both of Jacksonville, Fla., and Jaren (W.S.) Robertson of St. Simons and their five grandchildren were among those attending the celebration. Mrs. Jones is the former Miss Blanche Grimes. They are active members of First Baptist Church of Nahunta.

Left - 50th anniversary celebration in 1999.
Right - The happy couple on their wedding day December 30, 1949.

EPILOGUE

This book was inspired by the four handwritten pages
by Dad below as well as many interviews with him.

As I Remember
by Ben Jones

Beginning 1/2 century ago when I was eight years old living in Nahunta. Nahunta's main businesses faced the east west railroad which consisted of two general stores on the south side of the railroad located about where City Hall is now. The stores faced the railroad, one owned by Barney Strickland, the other by JW Brooker. The other side of the railroad track was the post office, Knox hotel, a store in between known as the Suwanee store and also a barbershop. Another store, the Petty store across the side street from the hotel where the Zippy Mart is now. The Petty store was a stop for me on the way to school if I had a penny (5 silver bells for a penny) made my day. This was the main street to Raybon and Jesup and just up by the school through the Negro quarters and by the railroad to Raybon as there was no 301. US 84, now 82, was in its present location, was rather new and it was paved. Two service stations about where the two are now, only they faced US 84, another service station and garage located in the point where Holts insurance company is now. The garage was Smith garage, Rick Smith's dad. Two auto dealerships, you could buy a Ford in a building where Brantley Gas is now. The Chevrolet dealership was located at the east corner of now 301 and US 84 owned by DL Jones operated by J Morris Highsmith. Nahunta lost their dealerships in the depression a little over 50 years ago. The store now known as A B Brooker and son was the old JW Brooker store which I earlier spoke of by the railroad track. It was moved approximately 50 years ago. One little story, yes I was fishing 50 years ago, at a bridge in front where Nahunta Parts is now. I caught a fish which was too big to pull through the crack in the wooden bridge. I went to the nearby service station and borrowed an ax from the late Mr. Pat Stokes. That hole remained in that bridge as long as it was there. For spending money I found old medicine bottles in trash piles and after washing them I would sell them to the two doctors which we had here at that time. They used them again. They paid me one cent per bottle. I also shined shoes and sold peanuts to make money at about 12 years of age. I delivered the Florida Times Union before going to school in the morning to 12 customers. I bought my own bicycle and begin working at my dad sawmill at the age of 12. We were using oxen to pull the logs out of the swamps. For entertainment we kids played marbles, played basketball and had a hoop tacked on the old garage at my house and used a rubber 8 inch ball. Claude Smith and I and others spent our spare time under that hoop. We had clay courts to play on at school. It was really nice when they built the first basketball gym. It was enjoyed by all. No TV at that time. My early years in school I was a good student but in high school I began failing and then came my first big mistake. I quit school. My advice to students, if you feel your grades are slipping don't be bashful about it, admit it and keep asking the teacher for extra help until you understand the problem. Most teachers are willing to do a little extra to help a sincere student.

World War II had begun at the time. I worked at the shipyard in Brunswick for a short time. They were building liberty ships to haul supplies and equipment to our forces overseas. Still at the age of 17 I joined the merchant Marines and helped sail these liberty ships until after the war. 14 trips across the Atlantic to Europe. The last trip we lost our ship to a minefield off the coast of Italy. Had to abandon ship during a storm.

Back in Nahunta World War II was over. I decided not to ship out again and help my dad run the ice business. People didn't have refrigerators or electric stoves then. Well that didn't last long. The war time draft was still in effect, they would not draft me as long as I was serving in the Merchant Marines.

After a year in the army and a stint in Japan, The army decided they wanted an all volunteer army so I had a choice, volunteer for four years or go home. It was an easy choice for me, goodbye Army, hello Nahunta. Most of the army boys were home now. Not all made it back. I pray that they are in heaven. The U.S. would pay us $21 a month for 20 months or until we found a job. Each month you would have to name four places where you had applied for a job. Well the fishing, hunting, ball playing that's what I was interested in so I qualified for only one $21 payment. I had a little money saved from the Merchant Marines, so I was in no hurry to get a job. Claude Smith and I did a lot of fishing and ball playing.

George Dykes got me started foxhunting when I was 15 years old. I guess he did a good job because I am 81 years old and I am feeding about 15 fox hounds now.

The most beautiful, wonderful girl in the world, while I was away in the army, a young lady from Brunswick after losing her mother, had moved to Nahunta to live with her Aunt Jewell Purdom and to finish high school. To make a long story short, we went to Hickox on our first date. They were having a Halloween party at the Hickox school. After about four years this young lady became my wife and at this writing, Blanche and I, we have been married 58 years and the above description of her still stands.

SOURCES

1. Google and Wikipedia

2. Excerpts taken from a story submitted to the Brantley County Historical Society by Frank Jones' grandson Edward J. Newton, son of Emmie Jones Newton, Frank's 6th child.

3. Dad's memories that he wrote and are included in the Epilogue.

4. Google

5. Google